21st Century Junior Library

WHAT DOES A MAYOR DO?

Kevin Winn

We the People: State and Local Government at Work

Published in the United States of America by:

CHERRY LAKE PRESS
2395 South Huron Parkway, Suite 200, Ann Arbor, Michigan 48104
www.cherrylakepress.com

Reading Adviser: Beth Walker Gambro, MS, Ed., Reading Consultant, Yorkville, IL
Content Adviser: Mark Richards, Ph.D., Professor, Dept. of Political Science, Grand Valley State University, Allendale, MI

Photo Credits: © Virales/Shutterstock, cover, title page; © Lopolo/Shutterstock, 5; © Ron Adar/Shutterstock, 6; © Salivanchuk Semen/Shutterstock, 7; © Sheila Fitzgerald/Shutterstock, 8; © Derek Hatfield/Shutterstock, 9; © Rawpixel.com/Shutterstock, 9; © Steve Sanchez Photos/Shutterstock, 10–11; © stock_photo_world/Shutterstock, 13; © CameraCraft/Shutterstock, 14; © Sheila Fitzgerald/Shutterstock, 16; © Ground Picture/Shutterstock, 19; © pada smith stockphoto/Shutterstock, 20; © lev radin/Shutterstock, 21

Cherry Lake Press is an imprint of Cherry Lake Publishing Group.

Library of Congress Cataloging-in-Publication Data has been filed and is available at catalog.loc.gov.

Cherry Lake Press would like to acknowledge the work of the Partnership for 21st Century Learning, a Network of Battelle for Kids. Please visit Battelle for Kids online for more information.

Printed in the United States of America

CHERRY LAKE PRESS

CONTENTS

WHAT IS A MAYOR?

The **local** government is the one closest to home. The local government runs your city or town. It makes decisions about things that affect everyday life in your city. These may include roads, schools, and businesses.

Many local governments are led by a **mayor**. A mayor is like the president of a city or town.

Some school districts are part of the local government. Others are run independently.

The president of the United States might seem far away, but a mayor is close to home.

A mayor is an **elected official** in cities and towns. The mayor works with the **city council**. This group of people runs the town together with the mayor. Some cities have a weak council and a strong mayor.

Eric Adams became the mayor of New York City in 2022.

Strong mayors make more decisions than the council. This is common in large U.S. cities.

Other cities have a weak mayor and a strong council. In these cities, the council makes the most important decisions, while the mayor's job is mostly **ceremonial**.

This kind of mayor appears at city events but doesn't make important decisions. In some places, the mayor and city council share power.

Mayors are elected by people who live in the city. A person who wants to be a **candidate** for mayor talks with city residents.

Ask Questions!

What would you ask someone running for mayor of your town? What would you want to know before voting?

Candidates share their ideas for the city. They ask people to vote for them. This is called running for office. It is also called a **campaign**. Voters choose the candidate they most want for mayor.

Voters can often vote in person at a local polling place or by mail.

WHAT DOES A MAYOR DO?

Mayors go to special events. They might give speeches or make announcements. They pose for photographs or sign important documents.

Some mayors have bigger jobs. They sit on the city council. They can approve new city laws. If they disagree with laws, they can **veto** them. They may lead the police department and fire department. They might also be in charge of roads, parks, and schools.

OFFICE OF THE MAYOR
Proclamation
FDNY Firefighter Darren Harsh Day
GET STUFF DONE
nyc.gov/getstuffdone
#GSD

Mayors do not make laws themselves. However, they can suggest ideas for laws. Mayors and city council members talk about these ideas at city council meetings. They might talk for a long time before they agree on the best idea.

City council meetings are open to the public. Anyone can go to the meetings. City residents can often sign up to speak at the meetings. They may be able to ask the mayor and council members questions.

When laws are passed, the mayor makes sure people follow the laws.

Look!

Find a news article about a city council meeting in your city or town. If you can't find one, look for one in a city or town nearby. What is the meeting about?

A city spends a lot of money. Schools need **funding** to pay teachers and keep the school buildings warm and safe. Fire departments need to pay firefighters and make sure the fire trucks work. Roads, train tracks, and streetlights all need to be fixed.

Firefighters are first responders. They keep people safe from more than just fires.

A city's **budget** is a plan for how to spend its money. In many cities, the mayor writes the budget. This job is important.

Think about your city or town. What would life be like if the mayor chose to spend a lot of money on schools but no money on hospitals? What if the mayor chose to fix the roads in one part of town but not another?

Make a Guess!

Make a list of five things that a city might pay for. What might happen if the city didn't pay for one or more of these things? Write a few sentences about your answer.

Each city and town is different, but many face the same challenges.

Think!

Imagine that you are attending the U.S. Conference of Mayors. What do you want other mayors to know about life in your community?

MAYORS ACROSS THE NATION

Mayors sometimes leave home to tell other people about life in their own cities and towns. They might talk to state or national leaders. They might talk to other mayors. Many mayors are part of the U.S. Conference of Mayors. Mayors in this group meet to talk about life in their cities.

When they work together, mayors across the country can tackle big problems. They might share ideas about **immigration** or gun violence. They can get new ideas to solve problems at home. They can also help national leaders understand what is happening in different cities.

The U.S. Conference of Mayors travels to events throughout the world. These mayors talk about things that affect people in cities around the world. For example, in 2023 a small group of mayors attended the **United Nations** (U.N.) meeting on climate change. They talked about ways that climate change affects their cities.

They shared ideas about how to help their cities deal with these changes.

Create!

Imagine that you are attending the U.N. meeting on climate change. Draw a picture that shows something about the climate in your city. It might show weather, trees, farms, or a body of water. What is one thing about this scene that could change someday?

ACTIVITY

WRITE IT OUT! What kind of person makes a good mayor? Write a list of five qualities a mayor should have. Name someone you know who has at least one of these qualities.

AID
FOR
LIFE

GLOSSARY

budget (BUH-jut) spending plan

campaign (kam-PAYN) the process of running for an elected position

candidate (KAN-duh-dayt) a person running for an elected government position

ceremonial (sair-uh-MOH-nee-uhl) without major power

city council (SIH-tee KOWN-sul) an elected group that helps the mayor run a city

elected official (ih-LEKT-uhd uh-FIH-shuhl) a government worker chosen by vote of the people

funding (FUHND-ing) money for a particular purpose

immigration (im-ih-GRAY-shun) coming to live permanently in a foreign country

local (LOH-kuhl) nearby or close

mayor (MAY-ur) an elected official who serves as the head of a city

United Nations (yoo-NIE-ted NAY-shunz) an international organization that promotes peace and understanding among countries in the world

veto (VEE-toh) to stop a bill from becoming a law

FIND OUT MORE

Books

Bedesky, Baron. *What is a Government?* New York, NY: Crabtree Publishing Co., 2008.

Christelow, Eileen. *Vote!* New York, NY: Clarion Books, 2018.

Let's Go Local!: Role of Branches in Local Government in the US. Baby Professor, 2022.

Websites

Search these online sources with an adult.

Local Government for Kids | Miacademy Learning Channel | YouTube
Learn how local government works.

iCivics
Find out how you can be an informed and involved citizen.

INDEX

ABOUT THE AUTHOR

Kevin Winn is a children's book writer and researcher. He focuses on issues of racial justice and educational equity in his work. In 2020, Kevin earned his doctorate in Educational Policy and Evaluation from Arizona State University.